Don't Give Up, Aaliyah!

Flora Ekpe-Idang
Illustrations by Bennie Buatsie

Copyright © 2018 by Flora Ekpe-Idang

All rights reserved. This book or any portion thereof
may not be reproduced or used in any manner whatsoever
without the express written permission of the publisher
except for the use of brief quotations in a book review.

Printed in the United States of America

First Printing, 2018

ISBN 978-1-7324220-1-8

Corage LLC
600 N 5th St
Minneapolis, MN 55401

DEDICATION

To my mom, Suzanne who encouraged me at every step of the way to pursue my dreams and get this book done. Your guidance, support, and everlasting love is why I want to be like you when I grow up.

To LaTonja, Gail, and Bennie that went on this journey with me from crazy ideas to crafting it into a mark left on this world.

To Ashley, a carefree old soul that sparked the character of Aaliyah.

To every Black girl that has inspired me, you prove why representation matters.

PART 1

CHAPTER 1

It is a typical spring day for the Martins. Mom is outside in the community garden just down the block from the family's Chicago brownstone. Dad and Omari are in the yard shooting hoops. The sweet smell of honeysuckles in bloom fills the air. Instead of being out enjoying the nice weather, eight-year-old Aaliyah is on the living room floor jotting notes in the little green notebook that she carries around everywhere. She likes being ready in case a good idea should pop into her head.

Dad returns from the park with Omari, wiping sweat from his brow. He shakes his head when he sees his daughter.

"Why don't you go outside, Aaliyah?" Dad asks.
"It's a beautiful day."

"I've got too much work to do," she says.

Dad plops down on the floor next to Aaliyah. He sees her drawing and making notes.

"What are you up to now?" he asks.

"I have an idea that's going to be a big hit."

Aaliyah is thinking about eating ice cream around the truck with her friends. They can't take their time and enjoy it. If they eat too slowly, the ice cream melts and makes a mess.

"Wow," says Dad. "That must be something. Let me see." Aaliyah covers her work.

"It's not ready yet, Dad." He rises from the floor. "OK, I'll wait for the great unveiling."

Aaliyah goes to her room. On the walls are posters of successful business people Aaliyah admires. It's her dream to be among them. She has not told her idea to anyone but she knows she will need help.

At school on Monday, she shows her idea to her best friends, Tara and Bee.

"What do you think?" asks Aaliyah. "It's a great idea," Bee says.

"I wanted to make something useful that helps people." "How are you going to make it?" asks

Tara.

"I've got the stuff to make the first one. I just need help putting it together."

"We can come over after school," says Tara. Bee nods. "Great!"

The girls meet in Aaliyah's bedroom to bring her invention to life. After hours of measuring, cutting and gluing, they finally finish. It is a long plastic tube that widens at the top.

"OK, let's go down to the kitchen and test it," says Aaliyah.

The three girls race down the stairs. Aaliyah runs to the refrigerator and pulls out a box of ice cream. Then she gets an ice cream cone from the cupboard. She puts the ice cream in the cone and puts the cone in the plastic tube.

"It fits perfectly," she says, beaming. Tara and Bee smile too.

Just then, Mom and Omari come in from grocery shopping. Mom places her bags on the kitchen table.

"What have you got there?" she asks. Aaliyah proudly holds up her invention.

"It's an ice cream catcher. It catches the ice cream when it melts. Isn't it great?"

"Uh, yeah," says Mom. "Except someone has invented it already.

"What???"

Omari, the six-year-old whiz kid, looks it up on his laptop. "Here it is on Amazon," he says.

Aaliyah, Tara and Bee gather around Omari's laptop and look at the picture.

"You should have looked it up, honey, to make sure no one else made it already," says Mom.

Aaliyah turns away and runs to her room. Her friends follow. When they get there, Aaliyah is ripping pages from her little green notebook.

"I'll come up with something better," she says.

Aaliyah turns on her computer and pulls out her little green notebook. She is determined to create something new that no one has thought of. She doesn't even notice when her friends say goodbye and leave.

At art class, Aaliyah notices something that gets her thinking. She notices how much trouble the children are having finding the crayons they want for coloring. The crayons are in a big box in the middle of each desk. The kids have to dig around to find the color they want. Some get frustrated and give up.

"I've got it!" says Aaliyah to herself. She goes home, pulls out her little green notebook and gets to work.

A few weeks later, Aaliyah is having lunch with Tara and Bee. She pulls her little green notebook out of her backpack.

"Here's an idea that no one has thought of. I looked it up this time," she says. Bee peeks.

"What is it?" asks Tara.

"I call it the Crayon Swiveler," Aaliyah says. "I got the idea watching the kids coloring in art class."

Tara and Bee look closer. "How does it work?" Bee asks.

"You decide what colors you want. Then, you put them into the Swiveler, up to ten at a time."

Aaliyah's friends smile and nod excitedly.

"Every time you want to change colors you pop the old one up, swivel and pull down a new one."

"Kids would like that," says Tara.

"Grownups, too; I read that they like to color to relax," Aaliyah says.

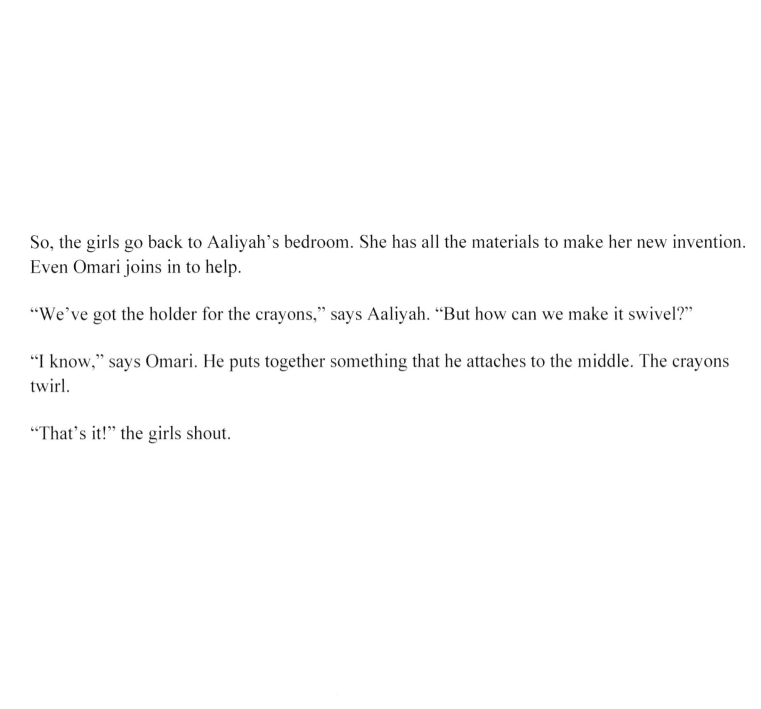

So, the girls go back to Aaliyah's bedroom. She has all the materials to make her new invention. Even Omari joins in to help.

"We've got the holder for the crayons," says Aaliyah. "But how can we make it swivel?"

"I know," says Omari. He puts together something that he attaches to the middle. The crayons twirl.

"That's it!" the girls shout.

They make a few more to test. Tara and Bee take their Swivelers home. Aaliyah has trouble switching crayons.

Tara and Bee call to say the Swiveler sticks. Omari comes down to the kitchen with a broken Swiveler.

"It doesn't work," he says.

In her bedroom, Aaliyah looks at the posters on her wall. She remembers that the business people who inspired her had trouble too. Cathy Hughes went homeless to keep her radio station alive. She believed in herself and didn't give up. Aaliyah decides that she won't either.

The next day, Aaliyah is tearing her room apart. She is searching for her little green notebook. She looks on her desk. On her dresser. Even under the bed. Aaliyah runs to the kitchen to ask Mom but she hasn't seen it. There are important ideas in it. She needs to see what went wrong with the first Crayon Swiveler.

"Have you seen my little green notebook?" she asks Dad. Dad walks over. He puts a hand on her shoulder.

"You're not giving up are you?" he asks.

"I don't want to. But what am I going to do?"

"What do you think?" "Guess I'll have to start over?"

Dad smiles. Aaliyah looks up and smiles too. "First, I have to get a new green notebook."

In her new notebook, Aaliyah writes down the problems she discovered. With the help of Tara, Bee, and Omari, she finds a way to fix each one. They get together and test again. It works perfectly.

Excited, Aaliyah goes door to door, selling the Crayon Swiveler, just as Madame CJ Walker did with her famous hair cream.

And, just like the hair cream, the Crayon Swiveler is a hit!

"We're so proud of you," says Mom. "Yes," Dad agrees. "You didn't give up."

Aaliyah smiles. She is already thinking about her next project.

BIO

Flora Ekpe-Idang was born and raised in East Orange, NJ and is first generation to a Nigerian father and Grenadian mother along with her brother. As the Founder and CEO of Corage Dolls: a toy company that helps to elevate, educate, and encourage girls of color to shatter societal barriers and be unafraid to embrace their full potential, she comes from 6+ years experience in advertising and multicultural marketing.

Having completed her BA in advertising from Pepperdine University, she garnered her MBA in entrepreneurship from Babson College. During that time, she became an award recipient of the Spark Pitch Competition at Harvard Business School, a Babson Social Venture Fellow, and a WIN Lab accelerator cohort member. Flora is here for the upliftment of girls of color, is a Black Girl Magic advocate, loves to travel, and enjoys four-hour karaoke sessions.

Made in the USA
Middletown, DE
19 July 2020